Digging a Hole to the Moon

poems by

Scott Noon Creley

Digging a Hole to the Moon

poems by
Scott Noon Creley

Spout Hill Press

First Edition
June 2014
Copyright ©2014 by Scott Noon Creley

www.spouthillpress.com
Pomona, California

Cover design by Ann Brantingham

Artwork for "Johnny and His Dog in Heaven"
by Johnnie Dominguez

ISBN-13: 978-0692232569
ISBN-10: 0692232567

For Carly

and

*for Mom and Dad,
Courtney, and Danny*

Foreword

Scott is impossible not to like. He was that way as an MFA student and he still is today. It's his absolute authenticity—he just doesn't know any way to be except himself—and it shines through his poetry as well as his personality. And when you're as talented and creative and experienced as he is, it isn't that easy to be that way. He and his poems are as thoroughly and sincerely compassionate—accepting—as you'll find anywhere in the poetry being written today, which is so often riddled with self-glorification or downright narcissism or, on the other hand, the attempts to escape other selves. Scott senses the world—human, non-human, and often simply inhumane, and takes it as it is—seeks its essences, its particularities, what Gerard Manly Hopkins called its "quiddity," into which we must "inscape." He understands it—or US—on our own terms--even as distant a people as those of China.

In literature, for instance, I'm kind of a Father/Son guy, as Hemingway was, as Turgenev was, as Sophocles was, as Shakespeare was, but Scott is more sensitive than Freud because he is more free of theoretical shackles, of the need to impose a scientific order on things. I love the pursuit of the genuine in Scott's "father poems," the complexity of the father, the understanding extended to him, the embracing of life in its wholeness, the originality that breaks through our stereotypes. It's the way the mind of Jesus worked, of Mandela, of Henry James, of Abe Lincoln. There's a vulnerability inherent in that acceptance of people, in the refusal to construct defenses around one's self or to launch psychological missiles at the fortifications that others may retreat to.

Also, of course, the guy can simply write—my guess is that he always could. He certainly could by the time he came to our graduate classes, and to the" little society" of like and unlike individuals of which, in Forster's sense, a writers' group is constituted.

Now he's a teacher, and I bet his students love him.

You're going to also, because he would love you.

Gerald Locklin
May 28, 2014
Long Beach, California

Introduction

To know Scott Noon Creley is to be amazed by his dedication to his work, his family, and society. He is one of the most socially conscious people I know, but his dedication to his fellow beings almost never manifests itself in words.

Scott spends his time doing what he can to change the world. For an artist, this means bringing arts programs to those who never would have been touched by them. He acts rather than speaks. He runs festivals for people in his community, magazines for teenagers, cultural arts programs for everyone. His life is a monument to his values, and he lives his morality.

This dedication to people has brought him in contact with the many of those who populate *Digging a Hole to the Moon*. It's a beautiful collection full of the humanity, wisdom, and beauty that defines Scott, but as you read his work, you should be ready to take put down the book for a moment, an hour, a day. He works with powerful and unusually painful subjects.

His community work has brought him close to so many people who have suffered, and Scott understands and feels their pain. At times, we witness the pain as so many of the people he is close to lose themselves to collisions or suicide. Scott does not shy away from their suffering or his own. He does not cover it in humor or gloss over it. This book is in part an attempt to understand it. He does not wallow; he internalizes. What we come away from this collection with is a kind of humanity ourselves. I doubt that anyone else feels the pain of others as deeply as Scott

Noon Creley. He distills that pain, allows us to understand it, and walking away from this collection, you will understand the world in surprising new ways.

I truly love *Digging a Hole to the Moon*, and I know you will too.

John Brantingham
May 29, 2014
Pomona, California

Table of Contents

I. Earthbound

Skin	19
Kaleigh	21
Two Cups of Tea Poured into the Grass	23
Origins	24
All the Hunger in the World …	26
Yesterday at Work	27
Why I Will Not Donate My Body …	28
Musculature	30
Leukemia	32
Starting Over	33
Fear	36
The Brain is Full of Electrical Impulses	37
The Last of It	39
Cold Confetti	40

II. Escape Velocity

Ontario is Tattooed With Maps of Itself	43
September 12th, 2001	44
Red Color News Soldier	45
Polaroid	49
God Gear	50
Ars Poetica Dentata	51
Our Non-Euclidean Lives	52
Novum	54
Welcome to Mesquite	55
Diabolus Ex Machina	56
Consider Smoking as an Equation	57
Color Theory	58
Launcelot in the Outbacks of Hell	59

Letter to the Victim I Failed   60
Good Times Nietzsche   61

III. Terminus

Ashes, White Noise   65
My Father at the Kitchen Counter   66
Biopsy   68
Elephant Gun   70
The Angel of Light and Ash   72
Epoch Coda   73
Prayer Watching   75
The Tunnel to Nowhere – Azusa, California   76
Grendel   78
Tres Retratos de Tres Hermanos   79
The Lives of Voodoo Dolls   81
The Moon is Down in Claremont   83
Ghost Words   Written Across Black Paper   84
Choking   85
Lapin   86
Sitting on the Hood of My Father's Car ...   87
The Faith Healer   88
Saints Who Are Lighter than Air   90
In Oak Park Cemetary, Claremont   91
London - The East End   92
Perfume Bauble   96

IV. (Trans)Lunar

Rooster   101
Johnny and His Dog in Heaven   103
Fragile Machine   105
If I Could Haunt You   107
Locked out of My Hotel Room in Zion, Utah   108

Memento Mori	110
Summer is Over	111
Starry Night	112
This is Your Lipstick	113
The Sun is Burning Hard	114
The Inland Empire	115

Earthbound

Skin

I left a shred of skin on the inside of my wrecked car, the
windshield scraping off the frill of my knuckle like a chef's knife
separating a piece of dough. The tatter of knuckle skin hung
there like frayed gauze, the limp discarded flag of a ghost ship.
It lost its color while I watched, changing from pastel pink into
a kind of mummified grey, severed from the blood and heat of
my hand. Uprooted and dying with the slow regularity of a
puddle growing stagnant.

The Jetta had rolled four times in the rain, gaining its tires and
losing them again like a wounded animal who does not yet
know it is dead. Although I saw the ground rushing up from
above, although a rock wedged into the open door and yanked a
handful of hair from my skull, I had not been hurt until I
brushed the inside of the windshield.

Now fluttering from the limp sheet of safety glass that droops
inward above the steering column, is this veteran patch of my
skin. Skin from the same knuckle that broke Brian Haster's nose
with the sharp, sudden motion of someone splitting firewood.
The same knuckle that has brushed the insides of parted thighs
and sometimes moved deeper, sending incomplete and
mysterious messages from beneath skirts and pant legs. This
same wrinkled thimbleful of finger that moves along the gentle
lunar incline of my girlfriend's face in the dark.

This overlooked piece of myself is hanging from a shard of glass
the size of a carpenter nail, finishing the parched business of
dying, and I am regretful. This knuckle that has brushed away
tears, has been cured like leather in paint chips and motor oil.

Now it will be replaced by something smoother, by the pink skin of new growth that cannot entirely be trusted, skin that I will have to build from scratch, that may not turn out as well.

And somewhere on the side of the freeway is that clump of my hair, maybe dyed black, covered in transmission fluid and tar, wrapped around rocks and tied into knots by the turbulence of passing cars. I hope that a few strands have been buffeted to other places, carried by the contrails of big rigs up into the Cajon pass to rest with the ashes of my cousin, wrapped around an axle and brought up north where a blue jay will put it into her nest, tucked inside the latticework of the Golden Gate bridge.

These silly dreams are important – because this skin is not going anywhere – it will be towed away with the car frame once I clean out my possessions. A secret bit of humanity tucked into the crushed hulk such places make of cars – hidden away inside the wreck we make of the world.

Kaleigh

Now that she is dead,
I sometimes see punk girls
with wide blue-jeaned hips or
in pink Marilyn Monroe sun dresses with big polka dots
walking down Second Street
and the adrenaline pours through me
sharper and faster than the way her mother howled
when they took her casket from the vintage hearse –
a car not unlike Kaleigh's '57 Ford Fairlane
except charcoal instead of robin-egg blue.

"Kaleigh was a classy, classy girl" her mother says,
once she has steadied herself,
Kaleigh's uncle holding her up by her arm.
All the kids at the funeral are wearing sunglasses,
running hands down their blue jeans
to erase invisible press-lines.
The kids still have their Mohawks,
peacocks preening at the edge of the grave,
blue hair gleaming under the hot hammer of the sun,
whose light is so bright and inappropriate against the black jackets,
vulgar where it glints off of safety pins
still dangling from hastily removed band patches.
My heart clenches and unclenches in the heat,
drowning in blood,
trying to squeeze it all out.

On the funeral booklets
wrung between black-polished fingernails
is a picture of Kaleigh.
It is her in the desert, broad and sepia toned,
beneath the same dry sun that's here at her funeral.
She is leaning against an ancient Corvette
black and bone smooth, so polished
that all the lights in the sky flare up in a second corona.
She is leaning back, porcelain hands in her pockets,

the insides of her thumbs touching the light tattoos
of vines scrolled across the dip between her hipbones.
Beneath the photo it says
"Give me a chance to shine and I will eclipse the sun."

There is a space inside of me
that collects guilty cobwebs and nightmares
like a fly strip.
A place hollowed out from being
the last person ever to speak to her
the last person who did not feel the flat static
creeping between her words,
the low sound of a faucet losing water pressure.
The person who did not see that her eyes were flat
like photos in week-old newspapers.
At least not until after the fact.

After the wake I handle her journal,
the one I know was hidden behind her
Misfits lunchbox.
I want for there to be no clues in it –
No hint of that silence suffusing
the calligraphy strokes in India ink,
or the black and whites of Audrey Hepburn
pasted around her poems.

If not here in the photobooth stickers,
if not under the cover of ticket stubs and programs,
then it was in that last conversation –
The coked-up boyfriend stories,
the tiger laying the shadows between palm fronds,
its stripes making it both hiding and hidden –
All of it
just another patch of sunlight and shade
springing out and pouncing
before my eyes could possibly adjust.

Two Cups of Tea Poured Into the Grass

Out in the garage,
under a dirty light bulb,
I read that the part of the brain
that holds the capacity for faith
has only the volume of a popcorn kernel.
This seed lights up for meditation,
for sweaty prayer or the low uneven gurgle
of a woman who speaks in tongues and retains
nothing of her ecstatic prayer.

This idea makes sense to me
because yesterday my father, an undertaker,
called and told me how
he guided two little girls to their parents' grave
where they laid out a blanket
and four cups of tea –
two of which they eventually poured
across the dead grass
just below the headstone.

With my eyes closed,
the phone humming against the side of my face,
I think that I feel that knot of cells
flaring to life in the salty nebula of my grey matter,
like a search light piercing
the water to find a destroyed car with two parents
but no little girls.

Maybe this clump of cells is like a signal flare
clawing at the sky in bursts of yellow and red
before falling back to earth and hissing out.
But possibly this knot is nothing
more than an exposed light bulb hanging in a garage
collecting dirt and the cooked skeletons of moths
until the wire inside snaps,
broken beneath the strain of constant illumination.

Origins

after Jeffrey McDaniel

I'm from hot rain scything over pavement,
sprinklers hissing in the silence.

I'm from sand stained pink
as it drinks up my father's blood.

I'm from .22-shaped holes in the sides of cars,
sun glinting off the flash.

I'm from sweaty hands running down her stomach,
clumsy saxophone harmonies drifting through the window.

I'm from knuckles
that still glow hot with contact.

I'm from eyebrows opened up for stitches,
the taste of blood between my teeth.

I'm from lies whispered in her ears at 4 am,
fingers sliding under the fringes of lace.

I'm from pill bottles
always growing empty.

I'm from orchards that run right up to the backyard,
the junkies stumbling through them in the dark.

I'm from hope
sliding sideways.

I'm from the rooster crowing somewhere in the next block,
cold mist halos in the streetlamps.

I'm from Catholic schools
with broken desks and cracked chalkboards.

I'm from lit candles,
cigarettes smoked on fire escapes.

I'm from the kaleidoscoping song of broken glass,
the laughter as we kick the door in.

I'm from words written backwards
on the insides of walls.

I'm from the orange light
threaded through apartment fires.

I'm from the sad smile of Father Tom,
the tremor in his voice.

I'm from my father's face in his hands,
the cop's palm on my shoulder.

I'm from the factory lights visible even in the hills,
arc sodium fire collecting in the night clouds,

I'm from my dead grandfather's switchblade
hidden up my sleeve *just in case.*

All The Hunger In The World Smeared Into Pigment

The redwood forest is the darkest place. The trees choke the light off early in the day. At night we stay close to the fire, tell each other stories about serial killers in low, splintered voices. Ten feet beyond the glowing liminal space around the burning logs there is just nothing, just imaginary line drawings and afterimages. I see haunted trees, grim cartoon wolves that flicker back between the trees after waving, darting into our periphery, letting their eyes catch the ember glare.

One morning, hung over, I wake up and walk to the bathroom to find a ranger standing over the corpse of a mountain lion, hands planted on his hips as if he might have snapped its neck himself. His eyes are inscrutable behind his cop glasses, they reflect the razors of light that cut between the trees and then slash the body, bisecting it into brazen gradients.

"Hit by a big rig," he says, although I didn't ask. Other people walk up now that I am standing there. Nobody touches it.

The mountain lion was golden, almost a hammered copper color. Its mouth was still open in a snarl, huge yellow-ivory teeth jutting outward like a dozen Sumerian swords, knives so sharp that they should have made the air bleed. Even so, it is the eyes that bother me. They are the eyes of a reptile, a stupid, endless green that fades down into black like all the hunger in the world smeared into pigment. These eyes are the color of leukemia, or maybe those of angels who are too disinterested to come when their hour is at hand.

Yesterday at Work

Yesterday in the bathroom there was a single tooth resting on the lip of the sink. It trickled blood into the bottom of the bowl the way that something thicker might run, syrup or honey. The tooth was almost white enough to blend with the porcelain, a small crack, old and brown, rolled across the middle – an injury from sometime before, one a dentist must have fixed. There is another smaller tooth, maybe half of one, sitting just inside the first stall. This one seems older, yellower, but must be from the same mouth.

I do not say anything. I lock the bathroom and hang up a sign saying "Closed." I hope that later tonight when I open the bathroom they might be gone. I ask every teenager if anyone has gotten hurt today, if anyone got hit in the mouth. Nobody knows anything, is missing any teeth. Someone pulled out two of their teeth and dropped them on the bathroom floor and nobody knows anything, saw anything. Not even me.

The janitors come and take them, but they sit inside my head for much longer, two little nubs of bone that lie broken on the white tile of my daydreams, an absence that I cannot help but probe with resignation.

Why I Will Not Donate My Body to Science

In her classroom, in the science lab,
Carly tells me, not looking up,
that the school is raising money for a new skeleton,
a human skeleton, held together with wires.
These cost thousands of dollars, maybe more,
the chalky weight of them, the craftsmanship
of their proteins laid across one another
like heady jewelry. The salvage of a life.

I lift up the arm of the old skeleton,
the one that needs replacement.
I let it fall. This arm, it could be three people,
the thick radius and ulna from a retired cop,
the cracked knuckle of a gymnast.
We do too much damage to our bodies
to use any one skeleton. I myself have
too many calcium stitches across my ribs
from kicks and punches I failed to block.
I have eroded the joints in my hands,
typing late into the night and drawing women.
I have jagged edges to my vertebrae,
the ones that cannot seem
to bear the dumb weight of my skull.

I could not be in anyone's skeleton.
I am too small, my bones, sometimes
they feel hollow, as if every day they
are sublimating, evaporating in the accumulated
glare of my heartbeats, withering from
the heat of caging me, the pushing and
expanding I feel inside when I read Eliot,
or hear coyotes howling in the distance.

I would not like to be that weak link,
the jaw that hangs too loose,
the spine that will not stand straight,
that hand that will not hold a fist.

There in the classroom,
while holding the bones
of so many people in that hand,
in my hand, I think it would be dishonest
to lend them my structure, to fool them
with the seeming solidity of me

because at any moment I might drift away,
might disintegrate and scatter into
crenelated pieces.
Then the gymnast, the retired cop,
they would have nothing left to hold them
to this earth, and we'd all be forced to stand there,
together, watching some school kid with detention
sweep us into the dust bin,

and I, secretly, would not be sorry:
these chipped teeth, the aching metatarsals,
I bought each one, and they hurt,
but they were me, when I broke against the world,
and it was beautiful.

Musculature

"You build muscle up by damaging
tissue and letting it heal," says Johnnie.
He switches pens, licks the end of one
and begins to make lines.
He has a porn magazine open on the table
laid out above the oversize paper and the box
of cheap Papermate pens, the only brand he uses.

The magazine photo is of a naked girl
bending over in front of a chair
half-turned away but looking back
almost shyly her hand raised to her mouth
one finger touching the corner of a fake pout
as if deep in thought, as if something
has just occurred to her in the moment
that the flash went off, the light
reflecting off the gentle curvature
where her ass meets her thin back.

"The scar tissue makes the fibers thicker,
strengthens the cords in the muscle
so that they can take more stress."
He works faster and her doppleganger
is emerging from the mist
of the paper in ink constellations of points,
hard black meridians and slashes.
On the page, she is less solid
than in the magazine
softened and ethereal.
As Johnnie speaks, as he sketches,
I picture the muscles in woman's back tearing,
the tiny fibers in her face bleeding microscopically
straining to keep that fake pout.
I know that the harm done here,

the intramuscular trauma,
it will make the next time easier.

The light from the hanging bulb
overlays the captured flare in the photograph,
the light reflecting off of her skin
now also the light in the studio,
two layers of false illumination,
an incidental gloss like a halo,
luminosity that suggests that what is
occurring here is perfectly fine,
that if we let the scar tissue collect,
we might eventually become stronger.
All we need is to be willing to bleed.

Leukemia

"This laryngitis is killing me, Scotty," says my grandfather, lashed to a hospital bed with plastic hoses and paper blankets. He says laryngitis instead of leukemia because of the morphine. I know I shouldn't try to correct him, but I'm confused and too young to believe someone when they tell me they are going to die, so I do.

"Leukemia," I tell him, "It's leukemia." The word has the weight of impending weather, it almost darkens the halogen lights for a moment. He looks frustrated, his skin turned yellow tissue paper wrinkling between his eyes. Then, instead of arguing, he just squeezes my hand with a hesitant kind of softness, as if to remind me that he loves me, even if I didn't turn out so bright. "Whatever you want to call it," he says.

Starting Over

My father was fired
eight months
before his retirement.
At 55 years old,
after thirty years working for Verizon,
He moved to Florida to sell graves
to people before they are dead.
He offers
headstones, land plots,
and funeral arrangements
tied together as neatly as
the newspaper wrapped belongings
that he has still not unpacked
into the small, empty beach shack.
He loses half an ear to skin cancer.
On the side of his head there is just
a shiny half-moon of scar tissue
where there used to be a Roman profile.
On the telephone, in the dark,
he tells me that graves are hard to sell,
does not say why.
"But still," he says,
"Still everyone dies, right?"
Far away,
his voice carried over
miles and miles
of telephone wire
"Sometimes," he says,
"you just have to start over."
As he speaks, I for some reason,
picture him selling grave plots
by thrusting handfuls of dirt
into the arms of the bereaved,
instead of speaking respectfully

of the departed
from across a mahogany desk.
I picture him sitting
in the center of his sand-dusted wooden floor
of the empty beach house a continent away.
The moving boxes are
stacked along his living room wall
like a row of newspaper-cloaked mourners
huddled around an open grave,
mourners to whom he must soon present a bill.

Fear

I see it in the sunset sky,
a bruised pink unfurling
into the dusk,
fading into a violet
that travels through the indigo sky
above creaking whispering corn fields.
It stretches back towards Florida
into a sky full of lazy yellow stars
that hang pregnant with humidity.
It drifts in through the window
and falls imperceptibly onto the skin
of my father's blue, stubbled cheek,
skin that will soon slide off under
a surgeon's scalpel
and then, once in the hospital furnace,
will twist back up toward
the moon as quivering ash,
that swirls just once before
it is pushed back down to earth.

The Brain is Full of Electrical Impulses

My father took me to work once,
into the switch room of the phone company
with wires hanging down over the circuit boards
like vines cascading down a fence,
their multi-chromatic flowers blooming
in frantic tangles climbing toward
the tops of the cold bricks.
This room was dangerous.
I could tell by the way he avoided
brushing any of the walls, his big frame –
hunched at the shoulders,
his arms stiff at his sides.
He was bent down among the copper smell
of live wires glistening over circuit boards
like flat emeralds.
When you touch a wire that might be live,
he told me,
touch it with the back of your hand
because as the electricity moves
through muscles it tightens them
can force your fingers into a fist around
the threads of metal.
I pictured frying to death
in the brick cellar of the phone company,
wrapping my hand around one of these bouquets
of live wires and clenching until
the backs of my eyes could see the blue fire
coursing in circuits through my iron-filled blood
and the wet thread of my muscles –
an unbroken circuit that would be a roaring sound
like waves breaking over rocks,
the sound of my synapses snapping apart
like overloaded breakers,
their small jolts made into one great depleted thought.

Maybe it is better, I think,
not to touch them at all,
that with a little planning this will be easy to avoid.
That such deaths are unique to electricity.
But seeing my father after the drinking catches up,
after the layoffs and the divorces,
seeing the way his hand perpetually tightens
around the bottle of Old Grand Dad –
I am afraid that I will someday
make decisions without knowing,
that I will extend my hand and find myself
locking my fist around something
that I was only meant to harness in small pulses,
enough ungrounded energy to burn me out forever,
the reverse of a divine word speaking clay into life –
a constellation flickering into darkness
subsumed by its own relentless mass.

The Last of It

The last of the liquor huddles there at the bottom of the glass, dirty gasoline waiting for a struck match. Some small pinprick of fire so that it can change from violent waiting into skin-blistering hurt. In two mouthfuls, I could be a different person, one who does not feel as if he is squeezing a handful of razors when he thinks about waking up in the morning. I am afraid of the impending years, afraid of the hurricane that will come and sweep me away if I do not hold my cup so tightly.

Cold Confetti

The glossy plastic had shattered like hard candy.
It mixed in with the leaves and grass on the freeway divider,
cold confetti as distant and inappropriate
as the numb heat of my fingertips
when I trailed them down the fragile architecture of your spine
and told you that I had just wanted to do something
that could never be undone.

Escape Velocity

Ontario is Tattooed With Maps of Itself

in drawings done in surface dust
an astronomical chart
marked by clusters of abandoned cars,
windows with cataracts of cardboard and tinfoil.
Broken glass is dusted across the asphalt
in inverted constellations,
miserly glitter that catches stray starlight,
then sends it back without answers.

The speed limit signs disappear,
speckled infrequently until they are lost altogether
in the warren of closed machine shops.
Those numberless little buildings hiding
between the patches of dry farm lot
that sprout corn-husk weeds,
like thirsty reaching fingers
that claw at the lights of low flying planes
but without drawing nourishment
from the hot dewy air.

This is a fringe place.
Here, I could hammer that gas pedal home
make my engine scream, and I could beat
Christ's own black mustang, the one
he'll ride back home again. I could race
the devil through the pale moonlight.
I could make that fucker dance.

I do, after all, know these streets,
these blind alleys and curves and potholes,
I know them the way you know
that quick sad twist in your gut,
the way you know that hopeless
way the muscles in your shoulders
will relax when its time not to bother fighting anymore.

September 12th, 2001

after X.J. Kennedy

The bodies falling from the towers
could be coins flipping end over end
through black smoke water,
could be hard blurry rain piercing
carbon saturated clouds to bounce off of
the pavement and shatter.

Could be anything but people
choosing the ground instead of the fire.
Later that night, near Cable Airport,
I sit will on the hood
of my Lincoln and marvel
that the sky is empty of airplanes.
I will think that the silence is starved
for the roar of a rotary engine
churning through thin, frozen air,
but that night, out in the black,
there are only the dewy afterimages
of satellites weaving in and out
of dim, ghost-story constellations.

Although I cannot see it,
I know those dim, blinking lights
are howling back digital echoes
of all those people plunging earthward,
a hard rain of ones and zeros,
their descent so absent of the merciful grace
of leaves shaken from a tree,
of a paper airplane swooping low,
of ash and burned scraps of paper
drifting to rest on rooftops.

Red Color News Soldier— Li Zhensheng

All female militia squad in Huteng Forestry Center. Feb 16th, 1976

In the photo, the women are crossing a winter clearing, their steps retracing a knee-deep furrow in the snow where the point-woman walked. It must be nearly nightfall, the shadows razored across the white forest floor are like slashes of unfurling black silk. The first three women have broken into a run, their rifles clutched mid-barrel like dance batons, held casually and not at all like implements for killing. One girl in particular, the second in the skirmish line, her left foot is leaving the ground in the beginning of a skip, her smile just a tiny crescent of teeth as brilliant and white as the snow at her feet. The women in the corner of the photo do not break rank, they hold their rifles at the shoulder, forever stern and ready to fire for Mao. There is a lens flare between the two groups, a spiritual dividing line captured as a flaw in lighting or focus.

Irrigation work camp on the Chaoyang commune, Heilongjiang province.
Dec. 17th, 1974

Hundreds of peasants and students are digging, so many that
the photos are in triptych. The canal winds across all three, an
impossible greyscale scar running from vanishing point to
foreground. The hole is so deep that it is never entirely out of
view, it carves a tiny chunk from the horizon, a fingernail's-
width of the print, which must mean miles in reality. This
absence is the subtracted mass of the earth added to that of the
sky, a conservation of matter. There is a balance here, achieved
in visual terms, an equality that all these blistered palms and
carts full of broken rock will never gain.
There are no mountains, no clouds – the dividing line between
earth and sky is just a variation in the gradient, recognizable
only in the irregularity provided by the canal. A single
loudspeaker is mounted on a post, almost out of frame. The
voice behind it organized all this. It is the sole point of order for
all the raw nothingness. There are tire tracks winding into the
horizon too, already faint. When all these people in the photo
are dead, this dry canal will only just have begun to fill. When I
am dead, it will have just begun to claim back snippets of the
sky.

Tienamen Square under review by Chairman Mao. Oct. 18th, 1966

This girl in the photo is dancing the loyalty dance. She is beaming, her hands and fingers touching the frame of the photograph, impossible to contain. Behind her, there are a hundred dancers doing the same, a thousand people past them, clapping all in unison. There are so many people that it should be stunning, overwhelming – this is not so. In the photo, in perspective, it all comes down to this girl in her soldiering uniform. She is a giant to the others, towering over the swarm of her cohorts with her face upturned and catching the light of the sun, her enraptured smile glistening under the cloudless sky. Her arms are thrown up so joyously to Mao, encircling the entire scene as if to say "Look what I have done for you."

Self portrait of the artist in a workcamp. Undated

Li Zhensheng is leaning against a tree and smiling at his illegal
camera. His coat and gloves look fine, clean even, not at all like
what they might give you in a prison camp. There is the little red
book of Mao sayings in his breast pocket, just over his heart.
The camera is set on the ground, tilted upward so it might only
look as if he were smiling, might be an illusion of perspective –
a natural function of light and shadow inverted first by his lens
and then later by my optic nerve. History reversed and reversed
again.

Polaroid

In the polaroid, you are staring over my shoulder.
The first delicate lines of sickness
are beginning to etch themselves into
the pretty hollows of your cheeks.
There is no hint of your coming radiance –
even with the sun is streaming through
your corn silk hair as it falls on your face
so that you are all blush and pale gold tones,
No hint that, as you collect yourself back,
you will smolder with grace.
You will become a lantern overflowing with fire behind dark cloth.
I would not undo any of the damage we have done –
not when it seems to winnow us out to be filled with better things.

God Gear

"They aren't really well built, y'know, under those cloaks"
— James Tiptree Jr. "And I Awoke and Found Me Here on the
Cold Hill's Side"

After the street races were busted,
in the makeshift booking station,
I am basking in the brief pulsar explosions
of the high-intensity-discharge headlights,
I am looking at my feet,
watching my shadow unfold
like a butterfly knife across the pavement,
flitting beneath each red-blue strobe from the cop car.
I am rubbing my fingertips together, admiring the feedback.
There is a heat, a subdermal sunlight, an opiate blush
to those hard-edged, Japanese-liquid-crystal thoughts –
The simple machine code
that pilots these billions of suicidal molecules.

Ars Poetica Dentata

When I write a poem, it is like pulling a loose tooth. At first, there is a low, itching ache, something slightly out of control in my bones. Something that has grown too fast, been jostled out of place. The wrongness is something my tongue returns to over and over, feels for in the dark of my mouth even when I am asleep. It distracts me from what I am thinking until there is nothing left but to yank and wrench. When I am done, there is an empty, bloody hole, and I have never been so relieved to have something gone. How could that tiny nodule of bone ever have lived inside of me, so malformed and eaten away, blacked with wear and so obviously not fit to live inside of a body? A loose tooth consummated in its extraction, complete only after it has been opened to the air.

Our Non-Euclidean Lives

"Theories! Pah! Those humans would draw maps through hell with their theories!"
—The Dragon, *Grendel*

It is so obvious we live in a curved world.
I can tell by measuring the ground
against the spike strip of the sky.
The clouds are gutshot but still climbing,
fighting to reach escape velocity
before the ionic feeling of dissipation
drifts through their gossamer cavities
the increase of entropy as snowfall feelings.
I imagine that they never do escape –
just loll and tumble through convective purgatory.

I have read that some black holes travel.
These cavities drift through systems,
pull stars from their spiraling points
(points that are not really fixed anyhow)
to make a bridal train of massive lanterns.
Points of light trailing a single aleph
of yawling darkness.

By noting the frequency
of the dishes piling up in the sink,
by graphing the scattered rabbit shit on the floor,
I can see that one of these rifts should be coming soon.
Instead of sweeping my eyes back and forth across
book pages intersecting the spine at cryptographic angles,
I should go outside and light a cigarette.

I should watch for the absence of light
wait for the red-shift in colors that will herald
the addition of another curvature
to the stuttering theorem that will pull us all along
into the leviathan vagaries of unanchored mass.

Novum

For James Tiptree Jr. (Alice Bradley Sheldon)

I watch that one video,
that one of that movie star burning to death.
The smoke a greasy curtain, the fire
seeming to cascade downward
like liquid seeking its level.
The sound is off. The egg-shell phone case is
hot in my hand, almost pliable.

When I click the screen black,
I can almost feel the itchy wire harness
on the back of my skull, the dumb tendrils
and filaments, the novum
traced invisibly into all those
jet black chinks and quivering wet fibers.

Welcome to Mesquite

The storm sent a bat spiraling
across the highway and ripped it
through the beam of my headlights,
its white skin lit so brightly that
I could see the
scrollwork
of veins inside one folded
broken wing as it plummeted
into the dark beyond the headlamps.

In the blackness,
the sand dunes
rolled soundless,
the dry particles swallowing
that bat as easily as it would water, as completely
as the charcoal rocks absorb the moonlight,
as my memory swallows
the shrieking I imagined,
the death cry buried beneath the wind.

Diabolus Ex Machina

I.)Boot sequence
I slide my fingers,
underlit in blue ghost fire.
Pentagram, pentagon, invocation.
Strum spinal chord, drum spinal tap,
dock spinal port. I want that copper-taste,
flicker-flash moment of cell-to-cell.

II.)Login
The sun is dropping into the flat grey clouds,
a drowning man dropping beneath the waterline.
The big bent-light sign for the porno shop
flickers to life, pink and ragged,
a defunct devil at an abandoned crossroads.

III.)dotHack
The entire polymer-slick, hard-ice surface of my display reads –
The wisdom of Solomon requires a sword.
I move my hands, just to feel the overlapping planes,
the interlocking fibers and restraints,
the *latency* of it all.

Consider Smoking as an Equation

as the math of bliss and agony.
The bartering of this future fifteen minutes of life,
for this five minutes of pleasure –
The algebra of cognizant addiction.
The alchemy of anti-smoking commercials
twining their dull punch lines with the sweet rush of nicotine.
It's the five minutes subtracted from the room
outside on the fire escape,
the scorching afternoon still lingering as heat in the wrought-iron.
It's the midnight wind turning up from the ground
across the sweaty, pebbled flesh of your shoulders.
Smoking is also five minutes outside of the funeral home,
when my friend's father has dropped dead,
and the day is so cloudy
and close to rain, but still muggy and hot.
It's three minutes staring into the tinted window at my reflection,
thirty seconds straightening the tie on my doppleganger,
that function of my raw-lunged sigh.
It is the dichotomy of gambling bits of life away
outside a memorial service
and being able,
with each drag, to arrive at the solution,
to feel the reasons that it is good to be alive,
even when my lungs are black.

Color Theory

Those poison colors
could be drawn
back out of her,
our lives together
undone
as quickly and easily
as wiping lipstick from my neck,
the only trace,
a slight redness
on my fingertips.

Launcelot in the Outbacks of Hell

His feet up,
taking his ease by the cold stone hearth,
Launcelot bounces a coin across the backs
of his craggy knuckles
with somnambulant ease.
He purses the wide, flat line of his mouth
and thinks that his only sin
had been to know exactly what he wanted,
and to have, at the last moment,
been too ashamed to take it.

Letter to the Victim I Failed

Dear Jane Doe,

I won't forget you. I heard you screaming, and at first I thought
it was a prank, your voice did, after all, have the high edge of
hilarity, for just a moment I'd thought you were catcalling me. I
even started to smile, but when you did stop, and when I heard
you pounding on the inside of the tinted glass, I meant to help
you, I did. I took two running steps toward you, then veered
toward my car.

It's just that I misunderstood, I drove the wrong way, and that
Jeep, the one belonging to your murderer, or rapist, it was gone.

Later, I told the police that the car was gold under the arc
sodiums. The waitress said it was black. Much later, they sent
up a helicopter, and I knew, as I watched the searchlight stab
randomly into the trees, that they weren't going to find you.

After the police left, after my wife went to bed, I turned out all
the lights and sat in front of my television, and I thought about
you. I watched a nature documentary, and I stayed very still
when a bristle-furred black wolf carried away a calf, and the
other animals just bellowed, knee deep in the snow, already
mourning their little baby.

I flicked off the television and sat there in the dark, crushing my
hands together, digging my nails in. I could imagine the rest for
myself.

Good Times Nietzsche

"Hey Freddy." I said, but Nietzsche, his face the poisonous white of milk and vodka, did not respond. He did not appreciate nicknames, felt they were demeaning. He lit up his pipe, and I wondered if maybe this was something I should do to improve the quality of my thoughts, get a pipe and smoke until my dreams emerged black and thick. I almost resented him for having it, the feeling settling into my gut like a handful of swallowed pebbles.

"Scott," Nietzsche said, "Do you ever wish you could be somebody else?" He stared off into space while he said this, stroked the fine-toothed comb of his moustache. I felt he did not see the sunset in front of him, its weak watercolor hues, the same way I did.

"No, Mr. Nietzsche, I don't," I said.

"Neither do I," he said, and pulled his lips back in something like a smile. He clenched his pipe stem between teeth, strong and long-lasting, monuments to a certain brilliant quality of despair.

Terminus

Ashes, White Noise

It is Ash Wednesday.
The children who walk by the window
have crosses smeared over their foreheads
in the thick pigment of burned palm fronds.

Those sigils are so rigid, so geometric –
Trailing down the sidewalk like a long line
of precisely punctuated speech,
a message that, for all its coherency
I cannot grasp before it trails out of view
around the corner.

Turning on the radio,
I want to listen long enough
to extract this same voice
from the ghost orchard of static,
my fingers twitching
at every tinny scrap of sound.

Here, with the blinds drawn,
with the glow of the television
pervading the room and mingling
with the blue onset of early twilight,
it is easy to envy those children their markings –
to hunger for the dead black certainty of them.

My Father at the Kitchen Counter

My father is a broken gunslinger,
his hands bunched into knots
that came from working too hard and fast,
as a soldier, as a hired gun,
half a world away from here.

In the white of his left eye
there is a tiny comet of blood.
A shattered capillary that hovers forever
just beyond the field of
broken blue ice that is his iris.

This blood star
blazes back in the dishwater light
of early morning
while he draws himself up
to his full height and grips
the edge of the countertop –

His face is filled
with the passages and furrows
that dreams carve
on their way out of the body.
His crow's feet are the fine webs
of glass freshly broken.

The spiraling torn edge
across his left cheek
was left by a stepbrother
who would never love him
and told him so while wearing his class ring.

The permanent darkness in the hollows
around his eyes are the tattoos
of affairs and addictions.
A litany of guilt drawn into
the bruised leavings of insomnia.

Propping himself against that counter top,
waiting for the coffee,
my father is somewhere else –
he is in the place that ruptures blood vessels,
that carves lines into wooden faces.
He is the last soldier alive on a beach,
a reservist in the south pacific,

The sole survivor,
ankle deep in scarlet water.
Each sigh makes his chest visible
between the lapels of his cotton bathrobe.
it is a Rosetta Stone for the translation of pain –
a language made up of the body
trying to survive the mind.

Each scar, each line of wear,
is a sentence in the prophecy,
of a man who does not yet know
that his ear will be amputated in six months,
that he will bury his mother in three.
They are the story of a life grown too heavy,
a weight still bearing him down.

Biopsy

After Richard Garcia

There is a place on my scalp
where the skin has begun to blossom
and unfold into a rose, a tiny scab.
I run my fingers through my hair
and feel its roughness.
I think of how rapidly it has changed
become an other, an unknown,
my own skin a liability,
a possible line in my epitaph.

As I read the braille of my scalp,
unwritten poems are scrolling
behind my eyes. A black man
sitting on a rock in Joshua Tree
beneath the darkening sky,
his face on his hands, the slow
hitching of his breath, the tears seeping
between his fingers shimmering in
the last of the evening light, blue and shifting
down towards red. He looks up
briefly and then continues to weep.

I see a flare climbing the night sky
in Yosemite, so bright my optic nerves shut down
and I see nothing, not even blackness.

In these unused images, these wandering ghosts
that may never be cleaned and chained,
are the wallet photo of dead teenagers,
There's Pauline, her cheeks blushing,
tendrils of midnight blue hair
tracing her cheek.

There's Devon Weirnke,
dragged to death across the blacktop
by his seatbelt,
the pavement a red streak, a comma that trails
toward the center divider.

In this marsh there is also Steve Bernstein,
my dead grandfather's best friend
as he, at my grandfather's funeral,
leans over the sink of a restroom,
grips the edge of the porcelain,
and struggles to pull himself upright.

There is my grandmother
dying slowly through a too-hot November night,
gray slivers of her hair scattered
like shrapnel across her pillow.

There is a green-handled screwdriver, magnetized,
clinging to the block of an engine,
dragged toward that distant twinge by a force
that will not, cannot, be dissuaded.

Elephant Gun

When I unsnapped the case, I thought it was jewelry,
the smell of metal polish like bananas, every inch
of gleaming chrome surface writ upon,
the scrollwork down the side of the barrel
like calligraphy, like vines, the thin lines
caught the incandescence of the single bulb.
The hammers were brazen, clockwork at rest.
The diameter of the barrel brutally wide,
the light seeming to disappear into the darkness
where I knew a shell could be sleeping.

I stepped backwards twice, almost fell when my
grandfathers old, scarred mason's-hand fell on my shoulder,
and he steadied me before I fell.
"I didn't mean to find it," I told him, and he folded his arms
old blue ghosts of tattoos rippling faintly with the vestigial
muscle, the lifetime of work giving him mass and gravity.
"Just close it up busyfingers,"he said, the ghost of a smile

because he hadn't been there the first time I'd gone shooting.
I'd absent-mindedly turned to speak to my father,
and also swung the shotgun
so that the barrel almost brushed his navel.
My father's broken-ice eyes went wide,
his hands flew uselessly in a cruciform
as if he were a magician about to abjure himself
from in front of the barrel. All of this happened in just an instant,
his lips parted slightly, his crooked lower teeth showed
and he gave a barely-audible exhalation –
"No."
And then I turned the gun away again,
and my father, seeing that I had seen his fear,
just told me quietly to never point it at anyone again,

never turn uprange,
but I started crying anyhow,
sat in the car and read the rest of the day
because in my mind I heard the gun go off,
I even remembered my father
telling me that nobody shot dies right away,
not like in the movies,
that anyone who is shot anywhere,
flops like a fish and maybe screams,
it they can still take the air in.
I remembered his far-away look,
as he told me this,
his third beer gone warm against his palm,

Back in my grandfather's guest room,
the elephant gun lay gleaming on the carpet,
spilled from its case, my grandfather smiled,
but his head tilted slightly now.
After his funeral I would look for the shotgun again,
I'd sift through the closet.
I'd find an old straw hat, a switchblade in a satchel
with wallet photos of he and a girl at 17,
but no shining rich-man's-gun that had never been fired.
I'd wanted to clean it, break it down, and let
the light catch the bore, cock and release the hammer
and hear the click. I'd wanted to pretend,
for a moment, that things
could be controlled in such a fashion,
that we could remain safe until we pulled the trigger,
that decisions could be separated from actions
by just the movement of a finger.

Angel of Light & Ash

He is circling in great raptor arcs
through the pink and orange watercolor clouds
that never had the right to exist outside of a Dali painting.
I have wept at the tight glassine arc of his smirk,
felt his cold, dry finger touch me on the temple
when he thought I might be ready to forget him.

I have learned to be afraid of him,
learned to notice that my stomach tightens when
his eyes, constricted with opiates, fall on the back of my neck.
It is not that he is there whispering in my ear
when they bury Kaleigh, nor that he snickered
when I finally recalled the sepia flatness of her last few words –

It is that I see him in all his quotidian awfulness,
in the symmetry of her ribs showing more and more
each hot day and dry throated night.
His subtraction of the world the inside of an urchin shell –
chamber after chamber coalescing with Euclidian cruelty,
proof tattooed over proof until the logic of it is meaningless.

He kisses her on the eyes when the headlights cross her face,
has the cruelty to make sure that
I see her smile in the dashboard glow –
not noticing the tires crossing the line just twelve feet behind her.
His wings flicker and fold in the smoke and hail of it all.
he takes away with one sketched graphite hand
and also takes with the other.

Epoch Coda

That night she took me into the desert,
so I could hear the low keening,
the trilobite hum. Their mindlessly sad
voices blended into the low susurrus
of souls flickering underground,
their glow drifting up from beneath rocks –
candles stifled by dark lantern shells,
a swarm of lunar-hued pinpricks behind clouds
the color and texture of steel.

I knelt at the bottom of the hillside
and put my hand into the ground, wrist deep.
They were dusty, blind, they brushed
against my fingertips then dove. Their glow
tracing through my veins for a moment,
up my arm and toward the shoulder.

I slipped my fingers around one,
my skin ghostly against its hardness,
his legs kicked as I drew him out,
it was like fishing, the way he struggled,
and I had to cup my hands around
the bruised glossy carapace. The way sand
trickled between my fingers like water,
the gravity inside of it wanting
the ground again, the cold deep fossil sleep,
the way a fish is drawn back to water –

Time is too fast for the dead here;
it grinds them down into fragments,
the wheel of a keymaker spinning
copper into sparks and powder.
She told me to let it go and I opened my hands,
saw one last black quicksilver flash

before it dove into the dirt again
the ground rippling, its little binary wheezing
blending back into the millions,
its song probably fading into genetic urges
and low unconscious cries as it plunged
back through the star fields of geological epochs,
past the stone orchards, past the angels
who fly upside down in the lowest gardens,
their hands like my mother's, the deep earth
worked into their skin like coal tattoos.

Prayer Watching

The Lost Boy does not like the viscous quality of prayers. He closes the panorama window. He lives in Park La Brea, often stands out on with balcony and watches the addict prayers rise like cigarette smoke, stretched thin and sometimes torn. To those who can see prayers, Los Angeles look like a structure fire. Prayers, much like pollution, are most visible at sunset and at dawn. To the Lost Boy, they look like milky gauze, like skinned ghosts twitching and shivering along the edge of the sky, clinging to birds and lightning rods like destroyed spider webs.

The Lost Boy is like a Hindu god, deathless, an adolescent kid who will live forever. He knows so many things now, looking out the window. He knows that past the orange sky, past the clawing finger bones of office towers, that the prayers will seep through the sky and dissipate. There are things that wait for prayers, wait and lick their lips. The Lost Boy does not like to think of these creatures fed, laying gorged on rooftops with their belts undone, picking their teeth with angel bones.

One of those prayers belongs to his friend, belongs to Sweeney Todd the Nightmare Magnet. Maybe another to the Hunger Girl. He does not look for these prayers, knowing the air would be too thick, that what the prayers contained might be too unsettling if he found them. He has shared the half-life of mythology with these people, does not like to learn anything new about them.

He closes the blinds and turns on the television, just for the noise. He does this slowly though – once you can see prayers you can see the other stuff floating around out there, animals slopped out of the salt-water tanks in hell, can see the Greater Monstrosities that roll over behind the hills in the dark. The nightmare magnet swears this is something blinking. The Lost Boy closes the blinds just to be safe.

Outside the prayers are tumbling around the street lamps like moths. They are a low insistent fog that settles over the sidewalk as easily as the muffled sobs come through the walls from the apartment next door.

The Tunnel to Nowhere – Azusa, California

The diggers wanted to quit
almost as soon as they'd started.
Their shovels broke on the rock.
Inside the cave, their breath fogged
if there was enough light.
And the cold –
The cold gripped like iron hands in the dark.
Breezes sighed up from the guts of the earth
and the workers slumped over, dead, choked on nothing.
Their hair fallen across their foreheads like sleeping children
tools still gripped in the loose circles of their fingers.
They quit, finally,
the only sound the toccata of loose pebbles
the crossbeams groaning in the dark.

In the dark of the caves,
just past the next few feet of rock,
the Cobalt people are still waiting
their hands clasped,
their skin shimmering with oil rainbows
in low the blue light.
Their arms are full of the strange, underground flowers
thin as rice paper.

The Cobalt people miss the distant twang
of picks against the ground,
the low percussion of demolition charges.
They are always hungry,
and they want to swallow ravenous mouthfuls of air.
They want to finally feel the warmth
of daylight on their cold, flinty skin,
to finally see the color of each other's eyes.

If they could dig with their thin, weak hands,
move that last few inches of earth,
they would see
that the sunlight is not at all like they imagined –
It is lighter than a spider's web,
it is everywhere at once,
ghostly as a song,
a rumor.

Grendel

for John Gardner

I cannot read *Grendel*
without seeing Gardner's motorcycle
scythe end over end onto the knife hot pavement.
I hope the dragon was not waiting for him –
that there was no voice brittle with laughter
to coax him relentlessly into the tooth-lined dark.

Tres Retratos de Tres Hermanos

"The Luchadore is wrestling with the Wrestling"
        after Lynn Emmanuel

Uno

        Rey Mysterioso, Monarch of Mystery, he is not receptive to grace. He is a deity who twists and snaps the hollow bones of angels, who loves the taste of his of blood when it gathers in coppery thunderheads on the insides of his lips. He is not receptive to grace. To divine mandate – but we do not know for sure. We never really see his face.
        Right now his pig-iron hands are turned palm up toward the hot lights, raised above his head and his muscles are not like a Hercules, an Apollo – this is a normal man who has rent down the walls-between-the-walls and now trails rainbow feathers where he treads. He shakes the earth when the balls of his feet leave the dusted canvas. And all this is with his bare hands, without him ever really letting us see his eyes.

Dos

What does it feel like to be the mask?
This vinyl armor stretching and aching,
aching to be stretched again over a roaring mouth,
to be strangling and unrelenting
in the midst of the fight – a necessary sacrifice
to help write a story where the other man's mask
is holding in his blood and spit,
like a second skin, the ruptured pulse
the stifled exhalations of pain just
beneath that second skin,
less solid than real skin
but more colorful, more easily identified.
So much more of a story than his face could be,
than your face, than mine.

Tres

He is off the ropes and twisting in the air,
reversing mid-sky like a hawk changing directions
his elbow is so rough, rougher even than his shoulders,
shoulders that know their work as fulcrums,
as axles and *axis mundi*.

Here he is in a poem,
a man who I imagine does not care for poetry –
unless it is the revolution of his legs,
unless the words describe the feline brutality of his feet
at first pointed at the sun,
then descending and becoming earth.

Oh. Dios Mío. Yes.
Tell me about the way he looked,
when he came plunging through the air down to the canvas.
Tell me he was a bullet, a falling raptor,
or even just a sparrow darting into a corona of sunlight.
Tell me he was your words dissolving into the jukebox music,
an image frozen on a screen forever,
like the red memory of my hand almost touching yours.

The Lives of Voodoo Dolls

Monday

His heart is a gris-gris
made of crow's feathers
lashed together with rum-soaked twine,
sealed with candle tallow
to the hard, opal molar
of an immolated saint.
Sometimes, in the morning,
if he leaves the house while the sky is still rain-soaked,
he feels those same feathers twitch and ruffle
still aching to unfurl after all this time.

Wednesday

He had accidentally slammed his fingers in the car trunk.
His simple wicker bones
had poked bloodlessly through his canvas skin.
Even though his fingers tilted like a falling fence,
there had been no pain.
Staring at his hand, he had wanted
to peel the seams that run up his arm,
had wanted to roll back the material
until he found the name painted across his insides.
He had wanted to know for certain
that somebody, somewhere else,
could feel this.

Sunday

His palms ache for a nail,
his teeth for pliers.
The difficult thing is not enduring the needles,
the lit matches hissing out in his armpits,

the bamboo twigs lanced beneath his nails.
The real difficulty,
is knowing that all of this direction,
this care and this planning,
the sing-song invocations,
the grunting, phlegm-choked curses,
the charcoal sketched hexes,
all of these things –
they really have nothing to do with him
are really only for the word written backwards
inside of his ribcage, the spurned lover,
the cheating spouse, the absent father,
the people who will be left
after he has been unraveled,
after the scores have been settled,
the tabs closed, the sins atoned.
His life has been nothing but a chit,
a marker, a curse whispered in the dark,
soft as the sound of lipstick grinding into a collar.

The Moon is Down in Claremont

and there is a ghost at the train stop,
an old black man leaning back in the bench,
a charcoal sketch in the pre-dawn light,
the white blur of a newspaper face down
in his lap. I do not want him to turn
to see his eyes, only whites, the color
of sun bleached teeth.
I stand behind him until
the train howls down the tracks,
heralded with red lights.

The old man is gone, the newspaper
still on the bench. I pick it up as
I walk past, the train is almost empty
an old woman sleeping on the second tier.

Looking through the window I can see
the moon is out again,
beside it are two other planets, glimmering
distant scraps of carbon and silica suspended flashing below
its dull weight, traveling despite their
stillness, rolling over out in the cold, spinning madly,
I know, even after they have vanished from my sight.

Ghost Words Written Across Black Paper

The Sumerians wrote names on everything – every brick had a god inside that needed to be named and cataloged. They tied ghosts to the most minor objects, scrolled Cuneiform down the sides and trapped whatever had the name inside of it. Nothing in my grandfather's secret apartment has a name. Not even my grandmother knew about this place until after he'd died. All the furniture is Macassar ebony, so black it does not even exist in the dark.

One of the last nights I am there, before I go out, I strip the stickers off of the leftover painkiller bottles. Vicodin ES, Dilaudid solution, Avinza extended release morphine tablets. They all have his name on them. If his ghost is anywhere I won't have it in these, these impotent confections meant to make the hollowing leukemia seem bearable, the drugs so thick and sweet they had him calling his cancer laryngitis the last time he spoke to me.

A bottle of his cologne is just inside the medicine cabinet. Even though the cap must have been on since his death the dry champagne smell of it is gone – as traceless as the odor of water. There are many things that take away. I suspect (smelling that the cologne has gone flat) that they far outnumber those that give.

Choking

My friend discovered his sister the morning she'd hung herself,
I imagine him
inching her door open and stepping into the room to find her.
Maybe with her tongue protruding thick and black as shoe leather,
maybe her fingers prying beneath the rubberized wire
of the phone cord looping over and over around her neck.
Maybe the faint swish of her dress as it swayed
back and forth with the dead weather
of the ceiling fan.

But here, in the gallery, seeing this drawing of her,
a sketch by her ex-boyfriend
I know it could have been worse,
her face could have been calm and placid,
her mouth closed, her eyes modeled slits, make-up still neat,
a death mask, her pores detailed so finely
that they faded into the grain
of the paper until the whole scene
became an intricate construction –
his sister's suicide made into an attempt at clever artifice,
a contrived scene,
a fiction,
but one that leaves him crumpled against my shoulder,
the thin cotton of my shirt twisting in his fist
as if he too were choking.

Lapin

"The cut worm forgives the plow" - William Blake, *Proverbs of Hell*

The rabbits are marauding, loose all through the house again.
This is not a good idea. They are cursed, possessed, or ill.
Wherever they go, they shit.
It is best not to look too closely at their leavings.
The pellets might take the shape of hanged men,
of gods clothed in flesh
hanging limp and broken from the crossbeams.
I do not turn my head
to glance at unusual movement
– When deep in its voodoo chants,
a rabbit will hover feet from the ground,
somehow smug, self-satisfied,
its tiny buck teeth glinting like arrowheads.
Rabbits engaged in debate turn nihilistic,
Nietzschean. It is easy to walk away,
to think that you have won the argument
only to find yourself, hours later,
in the tiny Italian restaurant in the village,
glaring disgusted at the
teenagers.
Do feed the rabbit, please, go ahead.
It will not be satisfied.

Sitting on the Hood of my Father's Car, the Night Before the Funeral

The desert above Rancho Mirage is so dark because there are so few city lights. We sit on the hood of the car, my father and I, and talk like strangers, groping for every word. It is too cold, the frozen ground is insinuating itself into our bones until they are no warmer than the shattered rocks heaved up through the sand around us.

I am twelve and I want to ask my father about Heaven. Instead I ask about aliens, flying saucers, if they could be real. He says yes, looking at me for only a moment longer than he probably meant to, lingering just a little because he knows what I am really asking. So I watch the sky for a while. Although I cannot tell the difference between stars and satellites, I know that I do not see any spaceships up there in the bleeding mess of nebulas that is the reservation sky. Nor do I hear any angels down here, picking their way over the rocky ground.

I am afraid for my grandfather, fearful that nothing will find him and carry him away. That it is too dark despite the stars and the frostbit desert moon, that he will be too heavy with the cold earth. I am worried that in the morning he might still be in that box, that he might have to be buried closed-coffin beneath the gloating Palm Springs sun. I would rather have him taken in the cold, before these very same rocks become embers and cook him into the clay forever.

The Faith Healer

I.
She hates to feel the wounds
knitting back together, pulsing
under her hands, thin threads of flesh
writhing invisibly across the pink divide
the secret palette of wounds, of cataracts,
the whistling echoes in punctures,
eyes glassy then cloudy again.

II.
In the field, she found a dead rabbit,
white and black, its flanks gold with dust.
She touched the nape of its neck,
let its cold, secret thoughts
flicker up her fingertips,
let the white-static
dead thoughts dissolve in the flame of her,
slow as ice in a hot mouth.

The rabbit's back legs twitched, its slitted eyes
opening wide, wider, mouth working
in the still wet morning air
as if it had found words,
but could not shape them,
tiny claws scratching pictograms in the
bluish earth between the shadows of the stalks.

III.
She, of course, has to bring the wounds back.
There is an equation to this world, a balance.
Cancer feels the worst as it returns,

when it blossoms back out again
in slow twitching heaves, black ink
through black water, shaking, sweating
venom. It reminds her that we
are all colorless inside, without witness
until we are open and under the knife,
the blessings and curses, all irreversible,
the words of them already long spoken,
thread dangling loose and ragged
in the eye of the mortician's needle.

Saints Who Are Lighter Than Air

The morning Kaleigh hung herself I remembered the story of a Hindu saint so divine she'd needed to be tethered to the earth to prevent her from floating away into the heavens. She lived her whole life like this – her toes drifting inches off the ground as her cold iron chains strained to hold her.

I imagine that my friend, the suicide, was the opposite of this – so terribly heavy and alive with the weight of only nineteen years that she'd had to suspend herself from the ceiling so that her hungry gravity could not crack the fragile eggshell of the world.

What did it feel like to have that mass building inside of her? How heavy was this density made of the early onset of twilight, half-smoked Marlboros, and unreturned phone calls? In the dream I make for her, the sky pulls her up up up once she has suffered for a moment, she and the saints twist around one another like dragonflies, like ribbons unfurling in a crosswind. I let her casket rest on my shoulder, keep my hands tight on the brass rail. The wind picks up, I almost feel it drift, so light she might have never lived at all.

In Oak Park Cemetery, Claremont

I line up little pebbles on the edge of her marker
so that their colors compliment the darker marble,
clash with the brass nameplate.

I don't know how many people
visit the graves of suicides, even one so nicely kept,
so carefully placed in the watery shade
between a few trees,
to keep off rain and heat,
both of which she never liked.
I can see her grave from up in the mountains,
so small that it is just like the pebbles
I put down when I visit.
From up here, the graveyard spoons against the hills,
green and naked and full to the brim of little white and black rocks.

When the sun begins to fall, when
the air rolls down, I want to go with it,
down over the white rocks that lead back into the city,
my feet just barely skimming the grass above her grave.
I want to swoop down, pick up a pebble
bring it back up into the sky with me,
a little piece of land cleaved from
the rest of the earth's dead mass.
I want to separate her out and elevate her,
carry her away from the burial plot
just two short blocks
from the house she tried so hard to leave.

London – The East End

The London sun makes grey light.
The air is already breathed,
stale and drifting above
the Georgian architecture
bolted over by incandescent chemists' signs
and the sightless retinas of satellite dishes.

The tube commuters just want
to get home without speaking,
but here, near Queen Mary's College
it is not so simple –
Not with the Hasidic graveyard
enclosed by a pizza parlour and billiard hall,
where pieces of stained glass
have been tread into the sidewalk.

Here, where they want to keep the ghosts
from their eyes,
not to see the new
wrought onto the bones of the old
with constellations of bolts
and gravid twists of fiber optic line.

Here, where the stone is polished raw
by the whetstone of footfalls.
There should be a riot of angels
working their way through the backlog,
ferrying armfuls of eroded souls
stacked like cairns.
They should be clearing away the foundation,

before the remnants can be built upon,
silted over by the sediment of new lives –

The Tescos bleeding display lights
on the walls of the Victorian pub across the street,
the band posters taped across the bubbled glass windows
hunching in their frames with age, their molecules
grown tired and plastic with the ages.

The church spires tangled with satellite uplinks
would be confusing to them,
the headlights reflecting in puddles could be mistaken
for the smoldering spirits of vicars and crusaders.

I visit the Tower of London.
There are concession stands
on the hanging grounds,
actors dressed in the felt
of dead soldier and vassals,
mock-fencing on the the gallow's-earth.

There is a chair made of knives,
a coffin out of razors,
poison suits of armor infused with mercury.
There is a wall that is filled
with baby princes.
Courtney, my sister, listens for them,
her corn-silk hair
trailing off the chalky granite bricks,
but her luck is no better than the angels,
and she hears no ghosts, no clue
as to where all these souls might have gone.

Beneath the floor of All-Hallow's Cathedral
there is a blitz chapel,
an alcove where soldiers could hide
from firebombs,
where they could try to pray
over the roar of incoming aircraft.
The altar is a small table of rocks
carved from the floor,
now surrounded by glass cases
full of Roman tiles,
lit by fluorescents fixed
into the raw earth overhead.

London is filled with places like this,
with secret rooms down stairways
whole lives of building and carving
hidden beneath just a few feet of rock,
perhaps a hardwood floor.
Like bone and blood
lurking just below the skin.

Beneath the chapel is a labyrinth,
a dark knot of corridors lined
with polished metal mirrors –
Someplace where soldiers starved
once their torches guttered out,
surrounded by dim outlines of themselves,
maybe cursing their own faces.

I do not know what might be beneath
the secret rooms, the leftover shrines –
Maybe just rock so lightless

to know it would be like
fingers tracing Braille,
the hand of a lost child
twisting along the inside
of a boarded up well.

But it seems there must be a cavity,
a container to hold the heavy mist of the dead
who would otherwise choke the air,
would ebb and flow into the city each night
like the tide of the Thames
drifting from the lipless mouths of dead men.

It seems as if we should have known
the consequences of so many lives lived in one place,
the relentless mass of so many prayers and thoughts.
It seems the angels should have warned someone
here where the world is almost worn away.

Perfume Bauble

I used to handle my mother's
perfume bauble,
It was a hollow glass gem,
the size of a robin's egg.
green as deep sea water
in the columns of sunlight
that poured between the heavy curtains.

I used to marvel at how that light
tattooed the skin of my palm,
a shocking heavy emerald
erasing the pale white of my palm.

Then I'd force the tarnished silver cap
listen for the exhausted shriek
the oxidized metal gave against
the degraded glass threads.

Then I'd pull in great gasps
of the the bone dry scent -
scorched cinnamon and tired citrus,

I'd search for my mother's ghost
between the swirling dust motes of late afternoon.

I held that breathe inside my lungs
until the sound of my heartbeat
became a tidal roar,
and, dizzy, I felt myself rise to meet her.

(Trans)Lunar

Rooster

(Animal Cops, Philadelphia)

After Kate Durbin

On the television screen,
I see a rooster hiding in the corner of the basement,
almost invisible past a column of sunlight that plunges
through the low window into the dust and shadow.
His comb is missing, red strip of skin where it should be.
He is strutting back and forth, pacing the small space,
a boxer ready to cross the ring.

The officer grabs him, and he gurgles, spreads his wings.
The feathers on his back are thin and white.
His left eye looks blind, a dead blue marble,
he stares into the flashlight.
This close to the camera,
I can see where the razors have kissed him,
linear divides in the feathers that show his pink skin.
"We have to euthanize birds like this," the cop says.
The rooster gurgles behind him, a weak protestation,
then gathers in everything it has, a crow, a roar,
that echoes off the plain concrete walls of the condemned basement,
the cop stops talking to the camera, just listens
to the last of the sound in the gloom.

"See me," it seems to say, "I was here.
I fought."

YES   NO

ABCDEFGHIJKLM
NOPQRSTUVWXYZ

1234567890

GOOD   BYE

Johnny and His Dog in Heaven

Johnnie gave me an ink drawing when he heard that my dog was dead.

In Johnnie's picture there is a dog strutting through the moonlight, clay cask of beer levitating in his paw, a jaunty top-hat with a peacock feather tipped behind his ears. Johnnie's Dog is on his back feet, dancing unsteadily, all his sharp teeth exposed in a bear-trap smile. A Ouija board has been superimposed over it all, the letters falling over Johnnie and his dog in organizing algebra, a system of coherent rules for star things and fever dreams.

I put the picture on my bookshelf behind Casey's absurdly-tiny pine coffin – the vet mixed rose petals in with the ashes, and I could not bear to bury them, not even in the backyard, beneath the flowers, just next to the hamster she had hated. It might have been a brain tumor, but I never had the money to find out.

In the picture, above the little coffin, conquistadors are winking down from their shadow castles, beards spun out of ink and cinnamon. There is a Eucalyptus tree creaking back and forth with the clouds. The earth curves away, small beneath them, its grassy horizon disappearing into the pointillist shadows of space. In every pen stroke, Johnnie and his dog are more dead, feral, elated to meet again.

Dogs, if they could talk, would answer the Ouija Board every time. Since Johnnie's dog can't, it waits just out of sight, panting and wagging its tail – waiting to see if Johnnie will come with it when he runs his next great circle around the twilight places it patrols in heaven.

At the bottom of the picture the letters of G-O-O-D B-Y-E loom large and plausible, urging for the marker to fall over their effervescent finality. If I could see them, I'd know that the ghosts of our dogs bounce grinning and predatory down the street outside my house, their ghost tennis balls hitting first the handball wall in the church across the street, and then plunking away towards Pomona, dissolving into the cold confetti of October leaves from the maple trees that line the avenue.

Fragile Machine

In the moonlight,
the bear seemed to boil up out of the shadows,
just darkness and gravity below the orange coal glow
of its eyes catching the stellar echoes of sunlight -
With my wife behind me, her back against
a tree trunk, my back pressed against her chest so hard
that the hammerstroke of her pulse thudded through
my jacket, beat time against my own.

We touched hands, and a brief arc of static
corruscated between her finger and my palm -
It seemed to flash
another layer of thin silver illumination
beneath the bright fat glare of the harvest moon.

For just a moment, the animal was outlined, visible,
up on its hind legs, its heavy skull
canted sideways, so that
it seemed asking an idiot question,
one that seemed to have no bottom
just a chuckling voice that spiraled,
repeating forever in the mossy animal clockwork
of its mind.
The short, wide trap of its mouth seemed to ask
"You? is it you?" with starving thickness,
voice choked with drool.

I imagined it would answer its own question by locking
its bone talons at the small of my back and unhinging
the wet trap of its mouth that had moments ago

almost curved sardonically at the edges
just a thin, smirking line of teeth showing until it yawls wide,
stinking of hot metal while it closes on my face.
My stuttering heartbeat, the fantastic whipcrack
surges of brassy adrenaline, raging up and down
the copper-wire clusters of my muscles now aching
with the urge to live past these seconds, even the flashing
waves of thought that imagined a nonsense question
emanating from –

All of this, the evanescent machinery of my life,
none of it had ever seemed to manifest
so clearly. Had never seemed so obviously fleeting
and brittle, ready to slide apart wet and tattered beneath
an undoing hand that might fall upon us as gently as our
fingers had met. Might be at once as simple and unknowable
as static gathering in the cold June darkness,
as brief as the glance the bear spared us before stalking away
without sound, without the sense of knowing how deeply
it had managed to strip us, the exposed gossamer
of our workings stretched and pinned beneath
the hungry, mindless question in those eyes.

If I Could Haunt You

I would like to guide you back awake,
to position the gray tilt of the light
against the cornflower blue linen
of your bed, the mosquito net frothing
over your gauzy silhouette.
You would see how bright the sky
was this morning, almost green, deeper
than you had ever possibly imagined
it could be. You would notice the sound
of water rising and falling in the marina,
the boats sighing up and down, steady as
a heartbeat. You would feel but not notice
the ghost of me, the love poem I traced
in your palm with my fingertip, one letter
at a time until it was written backwards
inside of you, something you would need
a mirror to read – the story of your cheek
resting flat on the pillow in the twilight,
your hair drifting on the dry midnight tides
of breezes and sighs.

Locked Out of My Hotel Room in Zion, Utah

Well after midnight, and I am sitting in a plastic chair, facing the edge of the desert.

The sky is mad with stars, big smears of galaxies that phosphoresce out there in the dark like sea animals in trenches. There is enough light to see everything, the sand piled up over the edge of the highway, dunes rolling over themselves as they swallow the trees arthritic with water starvation.

In one of the outdoor hallways there is a Pepsi Machine. I want a drink, but when I turn the corner there is a cascade of motion, the sound of rustling papers while a moth flaps its wings and climbs toward the ceiling. The moth is the size of a sparrow, is beating itself to death against the backlit face of the soda machine. It leaves little smudges of grey powder across the image of an icy aluminum can, drops minuscule feathers that drift toward the ground like sad confetti.

Despite his monster size, he has the same drives as any other moth – the strange need to dance and tumble near light, and he wants *this* light, the bulb behind the plastic. Because he is so huge, because I have never noticed that moths have tiny feathers, I want to let him reach it. I want to walk barefoot out into the sand and root around for a stone to smash the plastic. I want to spare him having to hear the hollow sound of his own body slamming against a barrier he can never cross.

I don't, though, I am afraid of what might happen. I don't know why moths seek light, or what they do once they have it. He might dive straight in, dive toward the light and just burn up on the bulb, his feathers – so fine they could be spun sugar – might just erupt in brief bursts of flame, sending him plummeting to the gum-stuck pavement, immolated in that last crazy instant of desire.

Instead of doing anything, I return to my plastic chair and listen to the doomed heartbeat, the moth funeral drum. I wait for the manager – confident that, soon, he will be back to let me into my hotel room, back into the dim circle of light from the bulb I see through the small crack between the curtains.

Memento Mori

"Old Man, 't not so difficult to die!" — Manfred, Lord Byron's
Manfred

There is a lump
one finger-length below my navel.
It aches, comes and goes.
Today, I will walk out to my car more slowly,
I will wink back at the red lights atop the water silos,
I will be grateful for the smoke and ash,
the distant fire smells.
In bed,
I will run my palm down
the gentle lunar incline
of your face, throw my leg over your hips,
will bury my face in the hollow of your collarbone.
My heart will beat arrhythmically
against the even tide of yours –
remembering.

Summer is Over

The trees outside shiver with its absence
and drop their leaves so hastily
that they seem almost eager to go to sleep.
The ground soaks up the cold.
It is thirsty for it –
The rock cracks and chips,
the flowers are sucked away
as gradually as they came
like fading photographs.
the birds are gone
one morning,
and we awake to silence.

Our house is unbearable,
without the benefit of a fire.
At night, we burn branches
and logs we buy from the store.
We wrap ourselves in blankets
and look out into the silver edged blackness
of the evergreen trees that cease to be green
in the early onset of night.
We do not notice as the ivy dies,
do not see that the flowers have gone,
that the bird songs are silenced –
We are too busy holding hands.

Starry Night

I want to live somewhere where the brush-strokes are visible,
the ebb and flow of the bigger picture transparent and moving
toward completion manifested in motion and in balance. I want
to live in a place where the link between each moment is both
logical and passionate, each clock stroke a splash of color in a
directed whirl of paint. I want to live in a place so obviously
mild and fertile, where the plants rise in silhouettes from the
patchwork hills, a place where the lights in windows are able to
burn clear and amber.

But foremost on my list of reasons are the stars, fat gas-lamp
galaxies hanging low over the tile rooftops, heavy with darkness.
Despite what the astronomers say, that some stars are long dead
and that we only see the afterimage of their lights, I know that
these stars will never go out. This night sky will always be
wreathed in the same burning pastel gasses, reflect the same
floral luminosity.

I will move there with my telescope. I will watch through its
lens and the rest of my life will come into view as surely as the
smell of honeysuckle froths over the purple hills and down into
the dark, endless valley.

This is Your Lipstick

This is the tube of lipstick that flew up
and hit me in the face when the car rolled,
that was sucked into the centripetal gyre
of our near-fatal event.
This lipstick bounced off my forehead
while I clenched your hand,
and the car slid backwards through the rain,
then finally flipped, dancing across the asphalt –
a skipped stone, a spent shell casing,
a coin down a wishing well.

You were not wearing this lipstick
the day the car flipped,
but still, in those last seconds,
the discarded tube reminded me of you,
pinging off my head,
sending shock waves
through the dense Jello-mould of my skull,
so that I remembered to tell you
"I love you,"
and think, I love your lips, and your lipstick,
and the way your hair became
a halo for a brief instant in the inverted cabin.

This is your lipstick,
it gave me the possibility of sailing from this world
with those pictures of you, those reminders,
to guide me somewhere else.
Before the tow truck arrives, I tuck it into my pocket,
hidden away in my those first moments of my new life.

The Sun is Burning Hard

The sun burns hard off the flat back window of a rust-speckled pick-up truck with spots like a robin's egg. The smell of wet pavement is like thunderheads, the potentiality of a secret force waiting to pour down the faces of the blue jean models on a billboard. We, all of us here, woke up and showered, scrubbed away the night sweats and oils, and are driving East now, out into the endless blue skies and sand plains. I am in love with this life, the gravity of it.

The Inland Empire

I.

In the dark cab of her Fairlane, I said
how all summer we broke windows for fun.
The pavement still sighing with midnight heat,
witch glow of the dashboard lights in her hair,
I whispered how the street races seemed to last forever
the screaming tires as mad and lonely as
the freight trains hissing and roaring through
the night between the empty lots and shops,
shooting toward the grim Los Angeles skyline –
the buildings like the slats in some great fence,
the barrier we were not fast enough to cross.

She was leaning backwards in her seat, head cocked
the firm white line of her neck plunging down
her cotton dress, the suggestion of her stomach
flat under the material, cotton catching
muted moonlight. She dangled one hand outside,
the cherry of her cigarette a spark hovering
inches from her thin fingers, a firefly suspended
in space, a still pendulum of light and fire that grew
bright and dim, bright and dim, codified certainties,
the morse code of a whispered scripture
that would never be written down.

In the car I told her how Joe Aguilera
pulled saplings from the ground, his eyes glassine,
predatory, his muscles shredding, his palms bleeding.
How, on fire with drugs, he walked down the island
in the middle of the street and destroyed everything
he could touch, howling machine laughter through

grinding teeth. How, the next morning, he woke up
screaming, some of his muscles worked off the bone
by his own strength. Kaleigh just leaned back in her
seat, eyes out the window, hands restless at the top
of her steering wheel, black nails fluttering toward midnight.

I tell her how my mother read to me, her thin arms wrapped
around me to reach the pages, the slow progression of
her fingers tracing the words, me in her lap the orange
arc sodiums tracing the paper between the blinds
because the lights were so low in the bedroom, her
breath stirring the hair on the back of my neck.
Good night Moon. Good night Clock. Good night Owl.
I say the words too, I sing them under my breath,
I feel her heartbeat fluttering beneath her gardenia skin,
a blood-filled metronome ticking against my shoulder.

II.

On cloudless nights like these, the lights visible
from the foothills, the darkness of the farms
breaking on the never ending warehouses
then against the greater blackness of our home,
I can hear Kaleigh's bones humming in her grave,
one long note twining over and over
sighing between cemetery willows
until it spills into my sleep, and I step out
onto the the porch and watch the smoke
swirl up into the watery air
evaporating before it has escaped
the halo of the streetlamps. Here the stars
sometimes form a fractured, half-blind cosmology.
I do not know their names and have not tried to learn them.

Mostly we disappear in cars. Mission road
winds dustily away into the flat amber knife edge
of the horizon. The street signs shimmering green lies.
Las Vegas, San Diego. The edges here curl inward
the circular logic of time and space, the lessons
we learn in the boxy trailer portable classrooms
now demonstrable in how we never leave but sometimes
vanish completely into folded metal of crashed cars.
The two objects wanting,
to occupy the same space, their matter intertwined,
the safety glass and plastic pushed into skin and hair.
But not Kaleigh, she disappears into the mute hollow
of a looped phone cord, her neck occupying the void.

In class our teacher shows us a looped strip of paper,
how if we trace it with our fingers, we could
follow it forever without breaking contact.

This is the shape of the universe she says,
eyes bright in the slate sky that blazes through the window

The roots of the tree in Joe's hands trace back toward the sky,
seeking rain in the dead heat of the night, their tiny
filament hairs twitching under the breeze. Joe's teeth locked,
he tells me that he knew it would be a boy. I am not
so sure. I will not watch this, will not watch his muscles
heaving and twitching beneath his shirt, sweat soaking
every inch of him until he glistens and shivers.
In my rearview mirror he is tearing at the ground again.
The lights of a big-rig trace a circle around him, his hands
at first touching the edges but then growing smaller,
less substantial, as if the light, like that strip of paper,
were curving too,
folding inward,
swallowing him whole.

III.
In June the birds sing all night, the street lamps are broken.
The house settles and moans, there is honeysuckle outside
and it froths indoors through the windows. I run my palm
flat across the stomach of a girl who never knew these people.
Outside a train is cutting through the night, a finger tracing
in the darkness but never lifting, moving through the silent hulks
of buildings in the distance, of empty lots filled with orchard ghosts.
It is a song from your car radio tuned between stations,
the snap and hiss shaping into your elegy. Good night Kaleigh.
Good night factories, Good night Los Angeles skyline.
Good night rabbits rustling back and forth in the hutch.
Good night ghost lights in your hair. Good night Joe, your
shoulders too big for my arms to fit around. Good night train.
Good night stars pregnant with darkness and nonsense omens.
Good night clock winding down, seconds always growing longer.
Good night mom, shadow traveling up the wall, growing thin.
Good night moon. Good night owl. Good night. Good night.

Acknowledgments

"Two Cups of Tea" in *Miramar* #2, June 2014.

"Lapin" in *Carnival Literay Magazine* Issue 1, vol. 2, 2013.

"Two Cups of Tea" in *Carnival Literay Magazine* Issue 1, vol. 2, 2013.

"Souls in Purgatory" in *Carnival Literary Magazine* Issue 1, vol. 1, 2012.

"Red Color News Soldier" in *Sentence* #7, Firewheel Editions, 2010.

"Skin," "Leukemia," and "Sitting on the Hood of My Father's Car" in *Bear Flag Republic* from Alcatraz Press, 2008.

"Starting Over" in *Mosaic Art & Literary Journal*, 2007.

"Addict Prayers" in *Freefall*, 2005.

Special Thanks to

Ann Brantingham
John Brantingham
Christopher Buckley
Jessica Drawbond-Page
William Mohr

About the Author

Scott Noon Creley holds an MFA in writing from California State University, Long Beach, and a BA in writing from UC Riverside. His work has been featured in the collection *Bear Flag Republic*, and in quality journals as diverse as *Sentence, Miramar,* and *Carnival Literary Magazine*. He was the 2014 writer in residence for The dA Center for the Arts in Pomona, California. He is one of the founding directors of The San Gabriel Valley Literary Festival, a non-profit that promotes literacy in Southern California with an annual festival and free writing workshops. He is also a digital artist and web designer.

Visit ScottCreley.com to follow his exploits and keep up with his work.

He lives with his wife, visual artist and photographer Carly McKean Creley, in Rancho Cucamonga, California.

CPSIA information can be obtained
at www.ICGtesting.com
Printed in the USA
FFOW02n0815091215
19470FF